CUBA

Paul Mason

Marshall Cavendish
Benchmark
New York

Other Marshall Cavendish Offices:
Marshall Cavendish Ltd. 5th Floor, 32-38 Saffron Hill, London EC1N 8 FH, UK • Marshall Cavendish International
(Asia) Private Limited, 1 New Industrial Road, Singapore 536196 • Marshall Cavendish International (Thailand)
Co Ltd. 253 Asoke, 12th Flr, Sukhumvit 21 Road, Klongtoey Nua, Wattana, Bangkok 10110, Thailand • Marshall
Cavendish (Malaysia) Sdn Bhd, Times Subang, Lot 46, Subang Hi-Tech Industrial Park, Batu Tiga, 40000 Shah
Alam, Selangor Darul Ehsan, Malaysia

Marshall Cavendish is a trademark of Times Publishing Limited

All websites were available and accurate when this book was sent to press.

Library of Congress Cataloging-in-Publication Data

Mason, Paul, 1967-
    Cuba / Paul Mason.
        p. cm. — (Global hotspots)
    Includes index.
    Summary: "Discusses Cuba, its history, conflicts, and the reasons why it is currently in the news"—Provided
by publisher.
    ISBN 978-0-7614-4760-3
    1. Cuba—Juvenile literature. I. Title.
    F1758.5.M37 2011
972.91—dc22
                                                     2009039862

First published in 2010 by
MACMILLAN EDUCATION AUSTRALIA PTY LTD
15–19 Claremont Street, South Yarra 3141

Visit our website at www.macmillan.com.au or go directly to www.macmillanlibrary.com.au

Associated companies and representatives throughout the world.

Copyright © Macmillan Education Australia 2010

Produced for Macmillan Education Australia by
MONKEY PUZZLE MEDIA LTD
48 York Avenue, Hove BN3 1PJ, UK

Edited by Susie Brooks
Text and cover design by Tom Morris and James Winrow
Page layout by Tom Morris
Photo research by Susie Brooks and Lynda Lines
Maps by Martin Darlison, Encompass Graphics

Printed in the United States

Acknowledgments
The author and the publisher are grateful to the following for permission to reproduce copyright material:

Front cover photograph: President Fidel Castro is applauded by a crowd in Havana, Cuba, in 2005. Courtesy of Reuters/
Claudia Daut.

Corbis, 8 (Bettmann), 9 (Bettmann), 15 (Blue Lantern Studio), 22 (Bettmann), 23 (Claude Urraca/Sygma), 27 (Jeremy
Horner), 29 (Reuters); Getty Images, 4 (Scott Warren), 6 (Stuart Fox), 7 (Hulton Archive), 11 (Time & Life Pictures),
12 (AFP), 13 (Gilberto Ante/Roger Viollet), 14 (Gilberto Ante/Roger Viollet), 17 (Hulton Archive), 18 (Hulton Archive),
19 (Hulton Archive), 20, 21 (Time & Life Pictures), 24 (AFP), 25, 26, 28; iStockphoto, 30.

While every care has been taken to trace and acknowledge copyright, the publisher tenders their apologies for any
accidental infringement where copyright has proved untraceable. Where the attempt has been unsuccessful, the
publisher welcomes information that would redress the situation.

1 3 5 6 4 2

CONTENTS

Glossary Words

When a word is printed in **bold**, you can look up its meaning in the Glossary on page 31.

ALWAYS IN THE NEWS

Global hot spots are places that are always in the news. They are places where there has been conflict between different groups of people for years. Sometimes the conflicts have lasted for hundreds of years.

Why Do Hot Spots Happen?

There are four main reasons why hot spots happen:

1 Disputes over land, and who has the right to live on it.

2 Disagreements over religion and **culture**, where different peoples find it impossible to live happily side-by-side.

3 Arguments over how the government should be organized.

4 Conflict over resources, such as oil, gold, or diamonds.

Sometimes these disagreements spill over into violence—and into the headlines.

"I realized that my true destiny would be the war that I was going to have with the United States."

Cuban leader Fidel Castro, interviewed in 2003.

A farmer in rural Cuba uses oxen and a cart for transportation. Since the early 1990s, Cuba has been short of gasoline—alternative forms of transportation have become increasingly common.

Cuba–An Island Hot Spot

Cuba is an island country in the Caribbean Sea. It has been a hot spot since 1959. In that year, the Cuban leader Fidel Castro came to power after a **revolution**. Soon afterward, Cuba argued with its powerful neighbor, the United States of America. In the years since, the two countries have often been in conflict.

Cuba is the largest island in the Caribbean. It lies about 93 miles (150 kilometers) from Florida. Cuba's capital city is Havana.

SPANISH CUBA

Cuba's people are a mixture of the descendants of black slaves, Spanish settlers, and other American and European immigrants. They are a living reminder of the different cultures that have played a part in the country's history.

Spanish Control

Spanish settlers took control of Cuba in the early 1500s. They forced the local people to be their slaves. Very few survived, so the Spanish began to bring in slaves from Africa. Today, many Cubans are descended from these Africans. Spanish control continued until the 1800s.

"They tell us, these tyrants, that they adore a God of peace and equality, and yet they usurp [take over] our land and make us their slaves."

The chief of the Taino tribe, which occupied parts of South America before Spanish settlement.

The Cuban town of Trinidad was founded by the Spanish in 1514, as a center for gold mining and farming. Today it is a World Heritage Site, with its old pastel-colored buildings, cobbled streets, churches, and squares.

Challenges to Spanish Control

During the 1800s, two groups of Cubans challenged Spain's control:

- Spanish families that had been in Cuba for generations, who thought of themselves as Cuban, not Spanish.
- Slaves and, after slavery was abolished in 1886, former slaves.

Until the late 1800s, the Spanish were able to crush all opposition to their rule.

Rebellion!

In 1895, another rebellion against Spanish control began. This rebellion ended in 1898 after the United States went to war with Spain. The Spanish lost, and after the war, a weakened Spain gave up control of Cuba. In 1902, Cuba became an independent country for the first time.

"Cuba ought to be free and independent, and the government should be turned over to the Cuban people."

U.S. President (1896–1901) William McKinley.

HOT SPOT BRIEFING

UPRISINGS DURING THE 1800s
During the 1800s there were four main uprisings against Spanish rule:
- 1823: independence campaign
- 1837: slave uprising
- 1868–1878: ten-year rebellion
- 1895: uprising that led to Cuban independence

Spanish forces surrender in Cuba in 1898, ending the Spanish–American War with victory for the United States.

POWERFUL LEADERS

Between 1925 and 1959, two men dominated Cuban life—Gerardo Machado and Fulgencio Batista. These leaders took a tight grip on power, and refused to allow any opposition.

Machado

In 1925, Machado was elected president. In 1930, he canceled elections that would have forced him to resign as president. The next three years were filled with violent clashes with his opponents. In 1933, army leaders told Machado that he had to give up the presidency. Without the support of the army, he had no choice but to go.

HOT SPOT BRIEFING

OPPOSITION TO MACHADO
What made Machado so unpopular?
- The falling price of sugar, Cuba's main crop, made many people poor. As leader, Machado was blamed.
- Machado reacted with violence to all opposition, making people dislike him more.

The Sergeant's Revolt

Soon after Machado had been ousted, there was **mutiny** in the Cuban army. This was known as the Sergeant's Revolt. One of the revolt's leaders was Fulgencio Batista. He soon became Army Chief of Staff. Because no leader could carry on without the army's support, Batista became the most powerful man in Cuba.

Colonel Fulgencio Batista poses in 1933, shortly before the Cuban army told President Machado that he had to leave office.

Batista in Power

From 1933 until 1952, Batista controlled Cuban politics, backed by the power of the army. Then, in 1952, it appeared he might lose control in an election. Batista and the army staged a **coup**. They made it clear that whatever happened in elections, Batista and the army still controlled Cuba.

Cuba under Batista

Under Batista, life was increasingly difficult for many Cubans. They were not allowed to disagree with the government. Food shortages meant that many people went hungry. At the same time, Cuba became a popular holiday resort for wealthy Americans and Europeans. Their expensive food and clothes were a big contrast to those of ordinary people.

Under Batista, Havana became a playground for wealthy foreigners. Many visited because they enjoyed gambling at casinos such as this one.

HOT SPOT BRIEFING

GANGSTERS IN HAVANA
- Batista allowed American mafia gangsters to open casinos and hotels in Cuba, especially in the capital city Havana.
- The mafia leader Meyer Lansky became one of Batista's personal friends.

REVOLUTION!

After 1952, Batista ruled Cuba as a **dictator**. He used the army and police to keep control. Those who opposed Batista were killed or imprisoned.

Arrival of the *Granma*

On December 2, 1956, a small boat called the *Granma* arrived in Cuba from Mexico. It carried members of the "July 26 Movement", which was named after an earlier revolt against Batista. They planned to start a revolution. Among them were Fidel and Raul Castro, Camilo Cienfuegos, and Ernesto "Ché" Guevara.

HOT SPOT BRIEFING

ERNESTO "CHÉ" GUEVARA
Born: June 14, 1928
Nationality: Argentinian
Ché Guevara met Fidel Castro in Mexico, and joined the 26 July Movement. He was one of the revolution's most important, and most **ruthless**, leaders. In 1965, Guevara left Cuba to support revolutions in Congo and then Bolivia, where he was captured and **executed**.

The Cuban Revolution, 1956–1959

BAHAMAS

N

0   50   100 miles
0   80   160 kilometers

Gulf of Mexico

Havana ⑦

ATLANTIC OCEAN

Santa Clara ④ ⑤ Yaguajay
CUBA

KEY
① *Granma* lands (Dec 1956)
② Revolutionary bases formed (1957)
③ New base formed (Feb 1958)
④ Captured by Guevara's forces (Dec 1958)
⑤ Captured by Cienfuegos' forces (Dec 1958)
⑥ Captured by Fidel Castro's forces (Jan 1959)
⑦ Revolutionaries arrive (Jan 1959)

Caribbean Sea

① Sierra Maestra Mountains
②
③ Sierra de Cristal Mountains
⑥
Santiago de Cuba

This map shows how the revolutionaries progressed from the coast of Cuba to the Sierra Maestra Mountains and on toward Havana.

The Revolution Spreads

Support for the revolutionaries spread from their base in the Sierra Maestra Mountains. They captured more and more territory. Several times they were nearly wiped out by Batista's forces, but they always managed to escape. By December 1958—two years after they had arrived in Cuba—the revolutionaries had Batista's forces on the run.

Batista Flees

On January 1, 1959, Batista left Cuba. The revolutionaries had captured several major towns, and were heading for Havana. The following day, Castro's forces entered the capital. The revolution had been successful.

Fidel Castro (standing under the lamp post, with the top of his hat visible) speaks to a crowd in Santa Clara. This photo was taken on January 1, 1959, the day Batista fled from Cuba.

CUBA AFTER THE REVOLUTION

After the revolution, Castro and Cuba's other leaders made moves to ensure that the new government would survive. People who might oppose the revolution soon found themselves under suspicion.

Purging the Army

The revolutionaries quickly began to **purge** the army. Anyone who might be an anti-revolutionary was forced to leave, imprisoned, or executed. Thousands of people are thought to have been killed during the purges, though no one is sure of the exact number.

HOT SPOT BRIEFING

LA CABAÑA
Many "anti-revolutionary" prisoners were held in the La Cabaña fortress in Havana. Conditions were harsh—the commander of the fortress was Ché Guevara, who was known as one of the revolution's most ruthless leaders.

Ché Guevara (on the right) speaks in 1960 to fellow revolutionary Raul Castro, Fidel's brother.

Defense of the Revolution

The government began to form "Committees for the Defense of the Revolution". Their job was to report anti-revolutionary activity and suspicious behavior. "Revolutionary militias" were also formed. These were armed groups of ordinary people, who would help fight any attempt to overthrow the government.

Land and Property Reform

Cuba's new leaders quickly began a program of land and property **reforms**. They began to nationalize Cuba's large farms and businesses. Even the farmland owned by the Castro family was nationalized. Large farms were split into smaller **cooperatives**, in which all the workers had a say in how they should be run. Many of these farms and businesses were owned by Americans. Others belonged to wealthy Cubans, many of whom fled to the United States.

"A revolution is not a bed of roses. A revolution is a struggle between the future and the past."

Fidel Castro.

Members of a women's militia go on parade in 1960. This was one of the first militias set up to defend the revolution from those who wanted it to end.

THE WORLD REACTS

The Cuban Revolution sent shockwaves around the world. In particular, it quickly brought Cuba's new government into conflict with its powerful neighbor, the United States.

Nationalization

Cuba's policy of nationalizing large farms and industries was very unpopular in the United States. By the end of 1960, foreign-owned farms, casinos, hotels, factories, and companies worth millions of dollars had all been nationalized. American citizens had owned many of these, and were furious at the loss.

Spreading Revolution

The United States and its **allies** (which included Australia, Britain, and New Zealand) feared that the Cuban Revolution could spread to other countries. The Cuban revolutionaries might encourage other **Latin American** countries to have revolutions of their own. If all these countries too were to nationalize foreign-owned industries, the result would be disastrous for any foreign country that had businesses in Latin America.

> "Our revolution is endangering all American possessions in Latin America. We are telling [Latin American] countries to make their own revolution."
>
> Ché Guevara.

In 1960, Cuban militiamen guard the entrance of the Texaco oil company in Cuba. The American-owned company had recently been nationalized.

The Cold War

The Cold War was a rivalry for power between the United States and the USSR (now Russia). At the time of the Cuban Revolution, most countries supported one side or the other. Under Batista, Cuba had been an ally of the United States. After the revolution, the United States feared that Cuba—which was right on its doorstep—would not be on its side any more.

THE COLD WAR
The Cold War began in the late 1940s and ended in the 1980s. On one side were the **capitalist** United States and its allies. On the other were the **communist** USSR and its allies. The two sides fought indirectly, by supporting rival capitalist or communist groups in other countries.

This Cold War matchbox from 1960 shows a communist fist smashing an American airplane. It was designed in the USSR to unite people against the United States.

THE BAY OF PIGS

By 1960, people inside the U.S. government were arguing that Castro had to be removed from power. They wanted him replaced with a more America-friendly ruler. Secret planning began for Cuban **exiles** to invade Cuba and get rid of Castro.

Invasion

The invasion attempt happened in 1961. The exiles landed at *Playa Girón*, or the Bay of Pigs. The Cuban government knew they were coming, and the Cuban army was able to trap the invading force on the beaches and in the fields nearby.

The Cuban exiles trained in the south of the United States, Panama, and Guatemala, before departing from Nicaragua to invade Cuba in 1961.

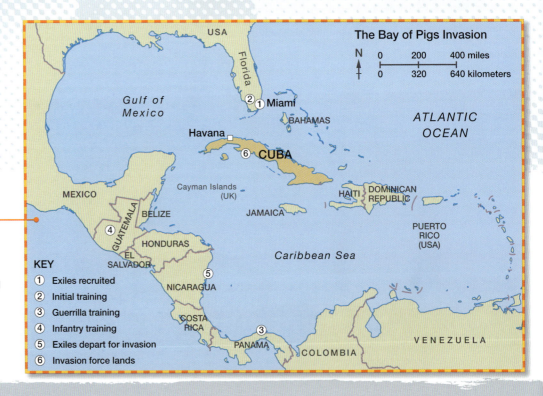

The Bay of Pigs Invasion

N
0   200   400 miles
0   320   640 kilometers

USA
Florida
Gulf of Mexico
Miami
BAHAMAS
Havana
CUBA
ATLANTIC OCEAN
Cayman Islands (UK)
HAITI
DOMINICAN REPUBLIC
JAMAICA
PUERTO RICO (USA)
MEXICO
GUATEMALA
BELIZE
HONDURAS
EL SALVADOR
Caribbean Sea
NICARAGUA
COSTA RICA
PANAMA
COLOMBIA
VENEZUELA

KEY
1 Exiles recruited
2 Initial training
3 Guerrilla training
4 Infantry training
5 Exiles depart for invasion
6 Invasion force lands

Surrender

Two days after the invading troops landed, they were forced to surrender. Although the United States had backed the invasion, helping to train the exile troops, President John F. Kennedy did not allow American aircraft to help the troops once they had invaded. Without air support, the invasion was doomed. Cuban forces captured or killed almost all of the exiles.

Results of the Invasion

The Bay of Pigs invasion strengthened support for the revolution inside Cuba. Even Cubans who had not previously supported Castro were angry that the United States had backed an invasion of their country. Some began to think that Castro's defiance of the United States was a good thing.

> "Thanks for *Playa Girón* [the Bay of Pigs]. Before … the Revolution was weak. Now it's strong."

Note from Ché Guevara to President John F. Kennedy, 1961.

Cuban army soldiers and militiamen pose for photographs after their victory against the invading force at the Bay of Pigs.

CUBA AND COMMUNISM

By 1961, Cuba had already begun to develop links with the communist USSR, the United States's biggest international rival. After the Bay of Pigs attack, Cuba itself would soon become a communist country.

Communist Cuba

During the early 1960s, Cuba began to adopt USSR-style communist policies:

- It became harder for people to own private property, such as houses, factories, or land.
- Property owned by religious groups was nationalized, and some priests were expelled from the country.
- The government took over all education, and banned private schools.

Reaction from the United States

The United States was horrified that Cuba was turning toward communism. It began a campaign of **sanctions**. The United States tried to persuade other countries that they should not trade with Cuba. If Cuba could not sell its sugar, or buy oil to make its machinery run, the country would soon fall apart.

> "I don't know whether he is a communist, but I am a *Fidelista* [supporter of Fidel Castro]!"

Soviet leader Nikita Khrushchev in 1961, after being asked if Fidel Castro was a communist.

Fidel Castro (on the left) joins the leader of the USSR, Nikita Khrushchev, for a meeting in 1960.

Help from the USSR

The USSR was delighted to have the support of a country so close to its rival, the United States. It began to give Cuba financial help, selling oil to Cuba at lower-than-normal prices. Cuba bought more oil than it needed, then sold the extra for a profit. The USSR also bought Cuban sugar, at higher-than-normal prices. These trades helped Cuba's government to survive despite the American sanctions.

Workers cut cane on a Cuban sugar plantation. From the 1960s to the early 1990s, the USSR helped Cuba by buying its sugar crops at a good price.

THE CUBAN MISSILE CRISIS

In October 1962, Cuba, the United States and the USSR were involved in a confrontation that had many people fearing for the future. For a few days, the world seemed to teeter on the brink of a **nuclear war**.

Fears of Invasion

After the Bay of Pigs, Cuba's leaders feared an invasion by the United States. The American **Congress** had authorized the use of military force in Cuba, and military exercises in the Caribbean Sea were planned for October 1962. Cuba's leaders decided that they had to be able to defend themselves.

Building Missile Bases

In 1962, work began on missile bases in Cuba that would enable Cubans to launch missiles at the United States. The missiles were being supplied by the USSR, and Soviet engineers were helping to build the launch sites. When the United States government discovered this, it told Cuba and the USSR that the missile bases had to be destroyed.

LAUNCH POSITION

MISSILE-READY TENTS

MISSILE ERECTORS

A 1962 spy photo reveals a missile base in San Cristobal, Cuba.

"[President] Kennedy was trying to keep us out of war. I was trying to help him keep us out of war. And General Curtis LeMay [chief of the U.S. Air Force] … was saying, 'Let's go in, let's totally destroy Cuba.'"

United States Defense Secretary Robert McNamara.

The Crisis Escalates

The crisis rapidly became worse. The United States would not allow missile bases that could attack American soil. The USSR refused to back down. For a few days in October 1962, it seemed that there could even be a nuclear war between the two countries.

An American warship intercepts a Soviet ship carrying missile supplies in 1962, during an American blockade of Cuban ports.

The Confrontation Ends

By the end of October 1962, the missile crisis was over. The two sides had reached a compromise agreement:

- The USSR agreed to dismantle its missile bases in Cuba.
- The United States promised not to invade Cuba, or help anyone else to do so.
- The United States agreed to dismantle its missile bases in Turkey, which could have fired missiles at the USSR, though this agreement was secret at the time.

CUBA AND THE THIRD WORLD

The Cuban revolutionaries had always hoped that people in other countries would follow their example. During the 1970s, Cuba began to encourage poorer countries around the world to have their own revolutions.

Africa and the Middle East

Cuba gave help to **anti-imperialist** fighters in several African and Middle Eastern countries. These included Algeria, Angola, Congo, Ethiopia, Mozambique, and Yemen. Sometimes Cuba sent machinery and weapons. Other times Cuban troops went to take part in the fighting.

HOT SPOT BRIEFING

ANGOLA
Cuban troops began fighting beside liberation forces from Angola (an African country) in the 1960s. The forces were trying to help Angola win independence from Portugal. Cuban troops also helped Angolans to defeat attacks by South Africa in the 1970s and 1980s.

Cuban soldiers, based in Angola in 1976, pay to have their boots cleaned by a local boy.

Latin America

The leaders of the Cuban revolution wanted to support revolutions in other Latin American countries. The United States opposed this idea very strongly. Nicaragua was the only country where a government supported by Cuba came to power. There, Daniel Ortega's *Sandinistas* toppled the dictatorship of Anastasio Somoza.

PLOTS TO KILL CASTRO

After the Cuban missile crisis, many Cubans believed that other goverments have tried to assassinate Castro in some bizarre ways:

- Poisoning his cigars
- Planting fake, exploding rocks at his favorite scuba-diving sites
- Sending him a bacteria-infected wetsuit as a present
- Poisoning the end of his fountain pen, in case he chewed it
- Poisoning his ice cream
- Some people even claim that there was a plot to send Castro an exploding cigar!

Fidel Castro shows his support for Nicaragua on a visit in 1985. He is seen here (speaking) at a Nicaraguan sugar factory, with President Daniel Ortega wearing glasses to his right on the front row.

1989: A WIND OF CHANGE

In 1989, a wind of change was blowing through world politics. The USSR withdrew its support for communist governments, and most of these quickly collapsed. Then, in 1991, the USSR itself broke apart.

Cuba Under Pressure

By the early 1990s, Cuba was under severe pressure. Cuba had always depended on help from the USSR. Without it, the government lacked money to buy goods from overseas. At the same time, the U.S. **embargo** on Cuba began to tighten, making it even harder for Cuba to buy goods such as gasoline.

Lacking gasoline, the Cuban army had to find new ways of transporting some of its guns. Here, anti-aircraft guns are being towed behind bicycles during a 1994 parade.

HOT SPOT BRIEFING

THE ECONOMY COLLAPSES
After the break-up of the USSR, the Cuban economy began to collapse.
- Imports fell by 80 percent. Cheap oil no longer came from the USSR. Food and medicines became scarce.
- Exports were also cut by 80 percent. The USSR no longer bought Cuban sugar at high prices, and new rules in the United States stopped even the tiny amount of trade between the two countries that had happened until then.

The "Special Period"

In 1991, President Castro declared a "Special Period" in Cuban history. Because Cuba could no longer buy goods abroad, it had to rely on itself as much as possible. Changes included:

- Transportation: people could no longer rely on gasoline-powered vehicles. Cuba bought more than a million bicycles from China, and also began making its own.
- Agriculture: every available space was used to grow food. Australian advisers helped to set up urban gardens on rooftops, for example.
- Power supply: Cuba began to develop wind, solar, and **bio energy** sources.

Castro's Health

In the early 2000s, rumors began to spread that President Castro was unwell. He seemed increasingly frail, and was seen in public less often. Then, in 2006, it was announced that his brother, Raul, had become acting president.

Fidel Castro's brother, Raul, greets a parade in Havana. In February 2008, Raul was formally elected Cuba's president. He had been acting president since 2006.

SUCCESSES AND FAILURES

At the end of Fidel Castro's presidency in 2006, the Cuban Revolution was 47 years old. What had been its successes and failures?

Survival

The Cuban government's biggest success is probably that it survived at all. The old revolutionaries are still there, and their ideas govern Cuban life. They have survived an invasion attempt, trade embargoes, and the collapse of the USSR.

Education and Healthcare

Although Cuba is a poor country, its education and healthcare compare well with the world's wealthiest nations. For example, a slightly higher proportion of Cubans can read than Americans. Cubans can expect to live on average for 77 years, compared to 78 for Americans.

Children gather outside a small school in Pinar del Rio, Cuba. Education in Cuba is free for everyone.

Shortages

Since the revolution, many goods have been in short supply in Cuba. New luxury items such as televisions, refrigerators, computers, and cars are unusual. Leftover 1950s American cars are still a common sight on Cuban streets. Even if new goods were available, few people have money to pay for them.

Restrictions

Cuban lives are restricted in many ways. Cubans cannot criticize the government. If they do, they risk losing their jobs, or even being put in jail. Few Cubans can own land or property, and they can trade only in Cuban pesos, the local currency. As a result, there is a big illegal trade using **tourist dollars**.

"All criticism is opposition. All opposition is counter-revolutionary."

Fidel Castro.

Old cars are still used in Cuba, years after they would have been scrapped in many other countries. These two are parked outside once-grand buildings in Havana.

CUBA'S FUTURE

Many people expected Cuba to change when Fidel Castro left the presidency, but most things stayed the same. Cuba's leadership still included many of the revolutionaries of the 1950s. So what does the future hold for Cuba?

The Death of Castro

Much has not changed in Cuba because many Cubans have a great respect for Fidel Castro. But his death could bring great changes to Cuban life. After his death, they may be less willing to put up with the shortages and restrictions of Cuban life. This could mean Cuba's government has to change.

Difficult Predictions

It is difficult to predict what Cubans want to happen next. The government always claimed that most people were happy with how they ran the country. But Cubans were discouraged from speaking to foreigners, so it has always been hard to know if this is true. It seems likely that many Cuban people would prefer to have more freedom than now—freedom to trade, own property, and say and write whatever they like.

"Fidel is Fidel, you know that well. He is irreplaceable and the people will continue his work even though he is not physically here."

Raul Castro, on becoming Cuban president in 2008.

A 'Victory Caravan' makes its way into Havana in January 2009. The caravan was a celebration of the day 50 years before, when the Cuban revolutionaries entered Havana.

Fuel for the Future

One area in which Cuba has prepared for the future is fuel and energy use. Many countries are trying to pave the way for a "carbon-free" world—a world where we no longer use **fossil fuels** such as oil. In some ways, Cuba is already prepared for this world. It had to stop relying on fossil fuels after the collapse of the USSR in 1991.

Solar panels are produced at the Ernesto Ché Guevara Factory in Cuba. Solar power is just one of the ways in which Cuba is replacing the use of fossil fuels.

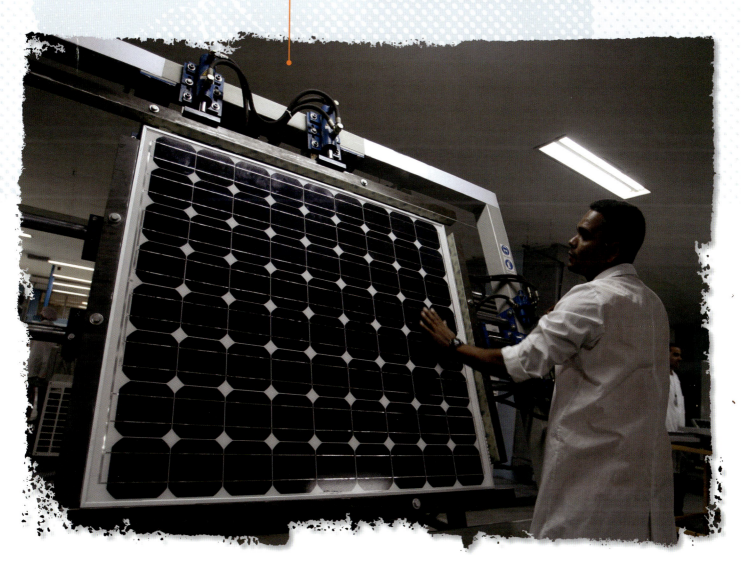

FACTFINDER: Cuba

Full Name Republic of Cuba

Capital Havana

Area 42,803 square miles
(110,860 square kilometers)

Population 11,451,652 (July 2009 estimate)

Rate of population change +0.233% per year
(2009 estimate)

Industries Sugar, petroleum, tobacco,
construction, nickel, steel, cement

Gross Domestic Product* per person US$9,500
(2008 estimate)

Percentage of labor force in agriculture 20%

Percentage of labor force in industry 19.4%

Percentage of labor force in services 60.6%

Number of phone lines 1.043 million

Number of TV stations 58 (in 2009)

> * Gross Domestic Product, or GDP, is the value of all the
> goods and services produced by a country in a year.
> (Source for statistics: *CIA World Factbook*)

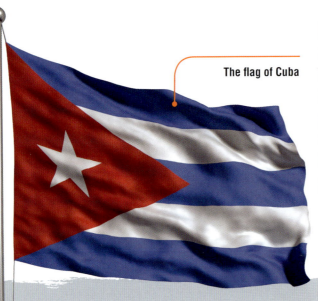

The flag of Cuba

FOCUS QUESTIONS

These questions might help you
to think about some of the issues
raised in *Cuba*.

Leadership and Government

How similar or different have the
leadership styles of Cuba's political
leaders been since independence?

Economy

How has Cuba's economy been
affected by its political relationships
with other countries?

Politics

Why have Cuba's political affairs
had such an impact on world politics?
How did the world react to Cuba's
change of government after its
revolution?
Why and how did Cuba support change
of governments in other countries?

Citizenship

Have Cuba's changes in government
been supported by its people?
How have the rights of Cuban
people been affected by its leaders
and their governments?
How has life changed for Cuban
people since the revolution?

GLOSSARY

allies groups or countries that work together or fight on the same side

anti-imperialist against foreign rule

bio energy energy from plant or animal materials

capitalist based on a system where people own farms, factories, shops, and other businesses, and run them with the aim of making money

communist based on a system where the government, rather than individual people, own farms, factories, and businesses, which are not run to make money

Congress part of the United States government that makes and amends laws

cooperative business that is owned and run by all the people who work in it

coup sudden seizing of power by use of force

culture characteristics that make a society or people distinctive, such as their language, clothes, food, music, songs, and stories

dictator person who rules alone, without being elected, backed by military force

embargo restriction on trade

executed killed as a punishment

exiles people who have left or been forced to leave their own country

fossil fuels oil, coal, and gas

immigrants people who have moved from one place to live in another

Latin America the parts of Central and South America that were once ruled by Spain, Portugal, or France

mafia secretive criminal organization in Italy, the United States, and elsewhere

mutiny rebellion by members of the military

nationalized taken over by the government

nuclear war war using nuclear weapons

purge get rid of opponents inside an organization

reforms social or political changes

revolution rebellion to overthrow a ruler or leadership system

ruthless without pity, or merciless

sanctions restrictions or penalties, threatened or carried out as punishment

Soviet from or of the USSR

tourist dollars special currency in Cuba, which is only supposed to be available to tourists. In fact, many Cubans have tourist dollars since it is hard for people to buy the things they need without them

USSR very powerful country that broke apart in 1991. Most of the USSR became the Russian Federation

INDEX